For Marlene

Adrienne Walker

M.D.
This book belongs to Marlene Bennett
This book started Dec. 1963

...

It now belongs to the
same girl, only her name
is Mrs. Marlene Robins
as of August, 1964

Dec. 4, 1963

Maturing Is Our Destiny

My name is Marlene Ruby Bennett. I am a 19-year-old young woman. I will be 20 years old on March 19, 1964. It will seem strange to not be a teenager anymore. Oh well, I can't expect to be young forever. I feel like a half-woman, half-child person. I guess most people have a little of both adult and child in their personality.

In spite of everything, I find myself maturing into a woman, with a woman's desires, interests, and thoughts. It's odd to look in the mirror and see a grown woman's body and face instead of a little girl's big-eyed freckled-nosed face.

Sometimes I feel like escaping back into my childhood because I had no worries, and was a completely happy child. Most of the time, however, I am glad I am my age because I am so much more free to do and say so many things. Sometimes it's actually fun to be an adult. Matter of fact, I get along better and feel more at ease with adults than anyone. Maybe that is because I am an only child, and was surrounded by adult relatives and friends.

I was always taught to respect my elders and I always did, and still do, if they deserve it.

A.W.

Property of Adrienne Walker

Nov. 2024

Nov. 2, 2024

My name is Adrienne Lela Walker. I'm 19 years old, born on March 19, 2005. This journal is a collection of entries from ages 15 to 19. Until now, I had kept them on my phone. But I realized that if anything were to happen to my phone (which has not been backed up in ages) I could lose a good portion of my writing. Having an analog version is an extra measure for my peace of mind. I can't remember most of the things I've written about. All I have to remind me of those past events are my personal accounts from when they recently happened, so I'd hate to lose them.

Feb. 1964

I am sitting on a green lawn with the warm sun on my back. A cool, almost chilly wind blows through my hair. The wind smells good and full of life-giving freshness. Everything around me is green, fresh and healthy: kissed by heaven's rain and nourished by the God-given sunlight. The season is late winter and the first signs of spring are appearing all around. The fruit trees are trying to burst into bloom with their blossom dresses. Tiny leaves peek out from the new branches of trees. The sun feels so good to me that I wish I could turn into a cat and roll on the warm cement.

When my body starts feeling the sun's warmth it seems to bring me out of my winter shell. I get a restless urge to walk or run and be youthful and young like a small child. My lips want to smile all the time. I want and need to go places, to be out in the sun, and to let it soak through my skin.

Beautiful weather makes me feel fortunate to be alive and healthy and be able to see and hear and feel the goodness of living in a beautiful world. I pity the people who are blind to nature's constant beauty. All my life I have noticed nature and therefore my life has been filled with more of what God meant it to be.

July 23, 2022

One school morning in May I threw on a crop top. It was finally warm enough to wear one and I wanted to show some skin. I walked into the kitchen for breakfast where Daddy was finishing up his. He took one look at me and blurted out, "You're looking a little pasty." I hate that word. He could have said pale, but pasty?

He was right though, I didn't recognize myself. From then on I was dead-set on getting a tan before the start of my senior year. I took walks and jogs in my sports bra and did all my outside chores that way too.

Last week, Denise and I went to the beach together where we made the mistake of not using sunscreen. The two of us laid out on towels to tan. I got up to look for shells after a while, and Denise fell asleep. When I returned 20 minutes later, she woke up red as a lobster and everything was painful. I don't burn so easily, so I was only a little pink.

A few days after our trip I noticed that my burn had transformed into a faint tan. I was happy that I had finally started to look like myself again. As a child, I had always been tan. I spent most of my time playing outside, and when I came indoors Mama would say that I smelled like sunshine. I wanted to smell that way again. My reason for tanning wasn't so much rooted in vanity but for nostalgic purposes.

April 1965

The weather has been very rainy for a long while. It has rained almost every day for about 14 days. It did rain for 11 days without hardly stopping. It has fascinated me every day. I have worshiped rain all my life. When I was a child I tried to get in the rain every chance I could and my mother would have to order me out of it. What a grand time it was when I had to walk home from school in the rain. What an exciting thing it was to accidentally on-purpose step into a huge puddle of water.

Rain always smells so good and fresh as it soaks the earth. The trees and plants seem to reach out for every drop. They sparkle and shine after the rain has washed away the dust. Then when the sun comes out all leaves glisten in the bright of the day. Things get water that normally suffer from lack of it.

Of course rain has its bad points. It causes terrible floods and ruins picnics and causes damage to many crops and other things. But I think rain does more good that helps man, more than to harm him. Without the sky's wonderful drops of water the earth would dry up and animals and people would crawl and dissolve in the dry dirt. I'll always love rain.

2023

On Monday it rained;

There was a puddle.

On Tuesday it was sunny,

And the puddle was still there.

On Wednesday it rained again,

But the puddle was gone.

May 1965

Sometimes I think I have such a sick mind. I seem to be afraid of everything almost. My greatest fear in life is people. Don't ask me why, I don't know. I have no reason to be afraid of anyone. Maybe it is because I am so sensitive. I have always been constantly on guard against people hurting my ultra-sensitive feelings. Also I have had a great fear of making a fool of myself in front of people. So I have always been uneasy and ill at ease with most everyone, and mostly people my own age or younger. I get along better with adults. I shall close this subject for now.

April 3, 2022

It isn't easy for me to get embarrassed at school. My shoes squeak, oh well. My legs stick to the seats, whatever. I bump into things, trip over stuff, cough loudly, correct wedgies, and leave sweat marks on the desks just like everyone else. But I didn't always think like this. I've come a long way to stop being so self-conscious.

In middle school, being an individual or even a human being was humiliating. I was laughed at and bullied for doing just anything. I didn't dress right, talk right, act right, run right, or walk right. And carefully calculating my actions made me look even stupider.

I still get self-conscious every now and then. It's a healthy amount. And I take comfort in knowing that probably no one remembers my embarrassing moments from middle school. That is, unless they liked me. When you like someone you pay special attention to their behavior.

May 1965

I have come to the conclusion I love animals much better than people. They are better and more faithful friends. They love you whether you're good or bad, smart or dumb, healthy or sick, pretty or ugly, rich or poor. As long as you love them, feed and care for them, and gain their trust, they are your friend for life.

I could not live unless I could have my beloved animals with me. I have owned so many wonderful pets in my lifetime and I intend to own and love so many more during the rest of my life. I can't understand why some people never have pets. I hate anyone who dislikes animals. I dislike very few animals. Even the ones I don't like can't help it if God made them mean. If people know these particular animals or reptiles are naturally mean, that people should completely stay away from these certain animals if at all possible. But most animals are not mean and if left alone do not hurt anyone. Animals can't help what they are. So I think humans should respect them for that and treat them accordingly.

One of the most awful things in the world is for an innocent animal to get killed. It hurts me so bad I get sick inside when I hear of an animal getting hurt or killed. I want to cry for each death. I could never ever ever kill any animal except in self-defense. I could not even kill a mouse. I don't see how people can harm an animal. I think anyone who hurts or kills an animal should be hurt in the same way. If I saw a person harm an animal I would pick up something and hit them. If I had my way, no animals would ever die, but if none ever died there would be too many to feed or care for I guess. I wish I could help and save all the animals I love.

Someday I hope to live in a place where I can own a lot of animals. I want to raise dogs. When I am an old lady I shall care for many pets.

I am thankful I married my wonderful beloved husband, Tim, who also loves animals and who is very patient with me with all my animal-talk and my pets. He is kind and understanding towards animals and gets very attached to his own pets. My poor dear Tim will have to put up with so many pets in our life together. I love my husband Tim more than I have ever loved anything. He is my life.

The Lord has been good to me. He gave me a good healthy body, good parents, good home, good life, good husband, good pets, good country, good everything. I thank God for so many good things he has blessed me with.

I hope the Lord forgives me if I have sinned in his eyes in my lifetime. I try not to ever be sinful. I don't want to be. My faith, love, and fear of God has helped me try not to ever be sinful. I am not mean and I have never been mean in my life. Maybe mean in small ways but never in intentional big ways. I hate mean and cruel people.

The Lord gave me the best, most wonderful, understanding, good, kind, smart parents in the whole world. I love my parents as much as a person could. God bless and keep them.

Dec. 29, 2020

Fifty-fifty

Fifty-fifty was a cranky old cat that belonged to my paternal grandmother's nextdoor neighbors. Fifty-fifty wasn't his given name. Grandmother called him that because he was orange and white like a 50-50 popsicle. She would leave food and water out for him, so he hung around her house often. As a child, I would play with Fifty-fifty all the time even though Grandmother told me not to because he would bite and scratch me. When he did, Grandmother would take me indoors and sit me on the bathroom counter. There she would dab a cotton ball with rubbing alcohol on my wounds to disinfect them. The alcohol stung bad and made me cry. Grandmother thought that was why my skin would get red and irritated. Nobody knew then that I had inherited my mother's severe cat allergy.

My reaction symptoms have worsened over time. I love petting my outdoor cat, but when she brushes up against my legs it feels like they are on fire. Itchy hives appear up my arms after holding her. I begin to sneeze constantly. My eyes water and itch like crazy and I rub them until they are red. The back of my throat will itch too. I'll scratch it with my tongue so hard that it feels sore like I've swallowed a cactus.

I'm a dog person by default, but I would like to be able to own indoor cats someday when scientists make a cure for cat allergies. Ideally, I would own all sorts of pets when I have my own home like dogs, cats, fish, hermit crabs, birds, frogs, millipedes, and scorpions.

May 1965

I love trees, grass, flowers and all that is green with all my heart. Give me the land that grows green and keep dry desert land away from me.

April 4, 2023

Going to Las Vegas in February was so much fun. I want to go in the summer next time. I haven't been able to stop thinking about it. I loved the drive there, seeing the desert environment with native cacti and drought-resistant plants. There was no humidity in the air, making my hair really staticky, but at the same time it had never felt so soft. I love the desert. Almost as much as I love the beach. They both have sand and strange plants and creatures.

May 1965

As of March 19, 1965 I was 21 years old, but it doesn't make any difference and I don't feel like it. I do not smoke or drink, so it does me no good to be 21. I wish my aging process would stop now. Now me and all my friends are beginning to age. That seems strange. It will be fun to watch all of us age together. I hope I don't age quicker than the rest.

Oct. 21, 2022

For the first 12 years of my life, Mama's parents lived an hour away and usually only visited on holidays and birthdays. They were almost like strangers to me. That was, until Grandpa passed away and Grandma had to move in with us because she couldn't get by all alone.

Now I have a very close relationship with Grandma. I assist her with bathing every week. She strolls her walker to the bathroom where I turn on the water and help her de-robe, step into the shower, grab objects, dry off, and get dressed. She doesn't like me looking at her body. She complains about her sagging and wrinkled skin. When she looks into the mirror she asks me, "Adrienne, who is that old lady? Certainly isn't me. I am a child at heart."

May 1965

When my husband Tim is not at my side I am lost and insecure. I adore the sight of him. I love his touch and his voice and the way he moves when he walks. He is my angel, my everything.

April 8, 2023

No matter where you are or what you are doing, just knowing that we are both alive and walking this earth at the same time gives my heart great fulfillment.

May 1965

I have decided that May is my very favorite month. In this month, one may experience all kinds of weather. For May is an unpredictable month. One day you turn the heater on and the next day the cooler. You wear shorts one day and a sweater the next.

Oct. 3, 2024

September is a perfect month because it's the mean of the two best seasons: summer and fall. It's still warm enough in the first half to go swimming, and in the second half it starts to cool down and everyone prepares for fall and decorates for Halloween.

May 1965

Now I will start the process of growing old. I have matured as much as I ever will. So now I shall watch the aging process start. But my heart will always be a child.

I have the best parents in the world. They have been so wonderful that I could not repay them back enough good if I lived 100 years.

Nov. 10, 2022

I love my parents, but I wish that they were more open-minded and easier to talk to. They can make me feel mad and hurt sometimes, but no one is perfect, and they are way better parents than most. I would not trade them for anyone.

May 1965

I don't get enough exercise. I don't know what is the matter with me. I ache like an old woman. As a child I exercised constantly. I regret that I cannot run like the wind as I used to. I wish I was a child.

Oct. 2024

When Covid-19 caused a nationwide quarantine in 2020, the only stimulation I had was social media and food. I gained almost 30 pounds in a matter of a few months. This horrified me. Grandma didn't let herself go until she was older, and here I was at a third of that age already on the road to destruction. I swore I would never end up in her position: overweight to the point of disability.

A combination of societal pressures in accordance with modern beauty standards and body shaming from close family members (both intentional and unintentional) made me feel like my worth was in my weight. The bigger I got, the smaller I felt. You could be the biggest girl and still not fill a room.

So before my junior year of high school started I went to extremes to lose the weight I had gained, that way none of my classmates would gossip about how I changed for the worse over quarantine. I lost 18 lbs in just a few weeks by means of extreme caloric restriction. This meant loss of muscle mass along with fat. I began to have a hard time doing physical tasks that normally didn't phase me.

To get where I am now (-30lbs from my highest weight) I have since engaged in extreme exercise, fasting spells, and extreme diets. These activities are always followed by binge-eating episodes, where I consume copious calories in a small window of time even when I'm not hungry. I fantasize about the same scene after every binge: me bent over the toilet with two fingers down my throat triggering my gag reflex. But no matter how strong the temptation I somehow never go through with it. And I will do anything shy of abusing laxatives to keep my stomach nice and flat on an important day.

It dominates my life. Every day I'm in a battle with my food addiction and my morbid fear of gaining weight. I have horrible intrusive thoughts and nightmares about me or the people I love eating themselves to death. But from the moment I wake up to the moment I fall asleep, all I can think about is when and what my next meal will be. My brain doesn't seem to realize that I'm not a starving person. I don't know that I will ever recover. I feel like a wilting flower.

When I look in the mirror I still see that larger version of myself. No matter how much weight I lose, she doesn't go away. Neither do the stretch marks or cellulite. I can never be satisfied. It's always, "5 more pounds and I'll have reached my goal." But the goal is always shifting: always out of reach.

Sep. 1965

This month starts a new school year. Just doesn't seem like I've been out of school for so long. Some mornings I feel as if I could just get ready and walk over to my classes with everyone. I can't wait for my class reunion.

2023

There were only four other people at Grandma's class reunion this year. She's survived a car wreck, breast cancer, influenza, and sepsis. It seems that she can overcome whatever is thrown her way.

Feb. 1966

Boy all the flowers on fruit trees are just a popping out all over town. I love blossoms on trees.

June 12, 2024

Butterflies flying:

A Corinna Daggerwing

Drinks from the blossoms.

Mar. 1966

I can't believe that this month I will be 22 years old.
That sounds so old to me. I was a teenager for so
many years. Now I have started the long process of
growing old. I wish I could stay 21 all my life. I hope
I don't age quicker than my friends. I will take good
care of myself so as to stay young as possible.

June 14, 2024

Time is fleeting, so it should be spent enjoyably while making the right decisions, otherwise it'll be too late by the time one realizes they haven't made productive use of theirs.

April 1966

I was just thinking, I bet people in the cowboy days of the west and even in early Victorian days must have smelled of body odor so bad that people of this day and age couldn't have stood near them. They didn't use deodorants, seldom brushed teeth, took baths, washed their hair or anything. But everyone else smelled alike so I guess no one cared. I can't stand anyone who smells bad. Now days there is no excuse for being dirty. There are too many good things to keep clean by. I try to keep my body, teeth and hair as clean as I can. The worst odor I think is stinking armpits and next on the list is dirty oily hair. There is no excuse for these.

2023

Anyone who gets within 3 feet of Grandma begins to choke and cough and desperately gasp for air because of the amount of perfume she wears. She sprays it on her neck, wrists, hair, and in a circle to form a cloud around her. I don't know how she can stand to breathe in such a thick mist, especially with her dog's nose. She says that she can smell a gnat fart. So why inhibit her respiratory productivity and drown herself in perfume? She must be insecure about possibly smelling bad. Or maybe she's creating a forcefield to keep other people's bad smells out. I wonder, if Grandma didn't wear perfume, would the ozone layer still be intact?

April 1966

Thank you Lord for giving me eyes, ears and all the rest of my good, healthy body. Eyes are the most important. Eyes to see life, nature, animals, sky, sea, land, people and everything. Thank you God for giving me eyes. Ears, ears are for listening to life, voices, music, animals, wind and everything which makes noise. Arms to reach, hands to touch and feel, legs to walk, run, dance, go anywhere. A voice to speak, laugh, cry, and say anything. A good healthy body to live, love, give life, feel comfort and pain. A normal brain to think, reason, plan, love, hate, and think of what it pleases. Thank you God for giving me my body and making it normal, healthy, and young.

April 3, 2022

Dear Jesus, I heard you pray for people, so can you pray for me too?

Dec. 1966

This year 1966 has not been a very happy year for both sides of my family. Especially sad for my parents and their separation. For me, my parents' separation has been unbearable.

In the past year I have found out my beloved Daddy is an adulterer. He's also a mild alcoholic. He has had one affair with cheap woman after another. This has been going on for 20 years. My mother suffered through these years without letting me know the truth about my Daddy. She knew how terribly hurt I'd have been if I'd known the truth. I am so very thankful she kept it from me. How brave she has been all these years. Now Mama is alone. She finally kicked him out of our home after I found out about Daddy. He would not change his evil ways so Mama could not take it anymore. No one blames her for that. She could take the liquor, but not the women. So now she is a very sad, lonely wife. But she does not want him back the way she had him — as an adulterer. If he ever comes to his senses and realizes how much he has lost I hope he will change and come home. How can he give up a perfect wife, a devoted daughter, a good family of relatives, a comfortable home and community respect for cheap women?

My Daddy is such a good man. He is honest, strong, hard-working, kind, neat, clean, sensible and friendly. But he has two terrible weaknesses—liquor and women. Why do most men have to be so evil and liars? Why can't they be faithful to their good wives?

I love my Daddy so, and I miss him walking through the house and seeing him cook and eat and play with the dogs. All the dogs loved him. I want my Daddy home with my Mama. That is where he should always be. I just keep praying and hoping he will change and come home. I will never be completely happy again until my Daddy comes home.

June 2022

Last Day of School

When the bell rang I walked out to the busses and couldn't find route 10. Jocelyn called me asking to save her a seat, but that's kinda hard to do when our bus isn't here. She found me outside waiting. We searched for 5 minutes, then finally saw our driver stepping out of an unlabeled bus to wait by the door. I complained, "We took too long. My seat is gone." To which Jocelyn replied, "No it's not. Just wait and see."

I always sit in the back left seat of the bus. It's my safe space. When I sat in the middle, people would throw stuff at me. That wasn't an issue anymore. I could see everyone and what they were doing from the back seat. I was protected from behind, and no one would dare do anything in front of the security camera right above my head. Every single day of the school year I had sat in the back so consistently that I stopped having to fight for it by being the first one on the bus, though I am most of the time anyway.

We hop on, and surprisingly no one is sitting in the back except for Axel stationed across from my reserved seat. I hate when he sits near me. He stinks of cheap deodorant and sweat. Axel is a loser sophomore with no friends. To compensate for his patheticism he does wild things to get attention. He dyes his hair crazy colors, makes suggestive gestures, and cracks misogynistic and racist jokes.

One time, last month, it was towards the end of my bus commute and us two were the only students sitting in the back. He tried to get my attention multiple times while I had my earbuds in listening to music. He shouted, snapped, and clapped as if I were a dog. I did not lift my head, so I never knew what he wanted me to see. That was until today when he started again.

I was curious this time, but I still did not want to give him any attention. So I opened up the camera app on my phone and inconspicuously faced it toward him. I recorded him while looking in the opposite direction. When he got off the bus I stopped recording and looked back at the footage. What I saw disgusted me.

His pants were unzipped, and he was holding his genitals. Did he want me to watch him play with it? Did he want me to see its size? I don't want to know. I was so disgusted with myself for being in such close proximity to him. Why me? Am I being punished for some sin I have committed?

Feb. 1967

All men are ignorant. It seems that married men are always chasing women. Why are nearly all men women chasers? I believe that most all men if given the right time, the right place, the right woman, will be an adulterer. I guess there are a few men who might have the willpower to say no. Why do men take a chance on hurting their wives and losing their home? We women have a hard time living with our men, but to me there is no life without a husband. And if a woman is single, life would be empty without a boyfriend. I'm glad the Lord blessed me with a good husband I love.

I don't like older men past 40 years. I don't know how a girl in her 20s could marry a man that old. He'd have to be pretty handsome and well-built for me to marry him. A man that old is already getting old and his body would not be firm and young unless he kept it young. I like young men preferably near my own age. A man young in body and mind. I like the thought of growing old together. I'm glad I have a young husband.

I like men with dark hair and eyes. I like a light or light olive complexion. I don't like a short man. I like no shorter than 5'11 or any taller than 6'3. Preferably 6' is perfect for my 5'8 height. I can't stand fat men, or a fat butt on a man. I love a tall, slim, trim-hipped, broad shouldered young man. Luckily my husband Tim comes close to exactly what I love.

Feb. 16, 2024

Today, Grandma asked me to describe my perfect love interest after she and Mama pointed out that I had never mentioned anything about boys or crushes. That's because it isn't any of their business. Mama has begun to assume I secretly like women. Women are attractive, but not my type. I would never date or marry one.

I'm attracted to these traits in a guy: medium length hair, small eyes, straight and white teeth if they can help it, skinny, 5'6 to 5'9, not younger than me, not more than 3 years older than me, hygienic, active but not disgustingly muscular or obsessed with fitness, doesn't drive fast or break traffic laws, doesn't engage in violence or commit crimes (besides vandalization for artistic purposes), respects women, doesn't hurt animals or insects, doesn't hunt or fish for sport, has no involvement with drugs, isn't an alcoholic, does not smoke or use any type of e-cigarette, preferably believes in God but does not suffer from religious psychosis, is not part of any cult or hate organization, is of sound mind, is not clingy, is not a picky eater, is not obsessed with football, is a great listener, is smart and creative, is curious and adventurous, is truthful and thoughtful, and is kind to all.

Any guy who fits this criteria is fit for me. So it seems I might be single for life because I will not lower these standards for anyone. A woman who settles for less than what she deserves does not respect herself.

Feb. 1967

I feel more at ease than most young people do when I am around adults. I can act and talk better. I do not feel at ease with people my own age or younger unless I know the persons very well. I feel young people are competing with one another most of the time. This is probably because I am an only child and I was raised around adults.

Dec. 2024

I would never date anyone younger than me. Men are already behind women their own age in maturity.

Feb. 1967

I get so disgusted sometimes when I can't find anyone to talk on the same level of knowledge concerning dogs. I love to talk about dogs. I know nearly every breed and study about dogs constantly. I just can't seem to find a person who is as interested or smart about the breeds of dogs as I am. Maybe one out of 100 people might know a little but not very many people know one dog from another. There are so many varieties to think of and love. There are so many breeds I'd love to own. I'll never live long enough to have all of them. Now I own two black poodles and a German Shepherd. I want an Italian Greyhound and a Newfoundland next. I also want a Japanese Spaniel, a Keeshond, maybe a Doberman, Greyhound, Collie and many others. I guess I'll try to have at least 4 dogs at one time or as many as I can. When I have small children I probably won't have enough time for more than 4 dogs. I have 3 dogs now to keep me busy. My beloved, Simone, Shawn, and Eve.

Nov. 29, 2020

Our mutt Shay had 7 puppies on the evening of Thanksgiving. I stayed up almost all night to make sure they were okay. I already have a favorite: a black and brown male whose father must have been a German Shepherd. He's the second largest puppy and the quietest. He sleeps all the time. I want to keep him so bad, but I'm afraid Daddy will say no and make me give him away. It's too late to not be attached to him. He's just so adorable when he sleeps in my arms.

...

Jan. 2021

Good news good news!!! Daddy finally caved and is letting me keep my boy! I named him Reno. Mama just bought a green collar for him. We have to housebreak Reno. He chews everything, including power cords.

Feb. 1967

I hate the desert. I want no part of it. It's dry, evil and boring. I know the desert has many natural beauties, but not as far as what I call beautiful. I love the hills and mountains where the Oak trees grow and the really high mountains where Pine and Redwood trees grow. That is the country I'd love to live in.

Nov. 3, 2024

All people seem to want to do in Central California is leave. They want to move to the South and live in cooler, greener places where it rains all the time. I love rain, but I also love hot weather, palm trees, tall grasses, tumbleweeds, cacti, cactus pears, succulents, lizards, snakes, and scorpions (when they aren't in my house). The skies here are almost always clear and the sunsets vibrant and gorgeous. We may have earthquakes, wildfires, and droughts, but we don't have to deal with tornadoes, hurricanes, huge thunderstorms, or snow (at least not in my city).

Feb. 1967

I love and watch T.V. so much I almost wish it had never been invented. It is a wonderful form of entertainment but a real waste of time. It is educational and I've learned a lot from it, but if the people wouldn't watch T.V. so much they would read and study more and be more well-read and intelligent. I certainly would. When I was in school I couldn't even study for watching T.V. I am more of a fanatic than most people. So is my husband and dad, but Mama just watches it when she wants to. Some people don't even bother to turn it on. I can't understand this.

2023

Ever since I was given a device to make videos with it was all I would do, and it is all I still do. I love to write scripts, act, and edit videos. I think I have been editing for a decade now. I'm no expert, but people say I'm very good at it. I would love to be a producer.

Feb. 1967

I have a phobia of silence. I hate silence. I either have to have the T.V., radio, or record player going at all times whether I am listening or watching it at all. I just have to have noise of some kind. My nerves are shot when it is quiet. I guess a great torture to me would be to put me in a silent room all day. I wonder why I'm like that? I even like to go to sleep with noise and lights on. Too bright of me I guess? Haha. I love to fall asleep on the couch with a light on my face and the T.V. on. Guess I'm just a nut.

Dec. 9, 2023

I am terrified of anything that flies and stings. In the backyard of my childhood home was a huge rosemary bush. There would be hundreds of bees gathering pollen from it in the spring and summer. If I got too close they would invade my personal space or "chase" me back inside the house. Wasps are the worst though. Their alarming colors, long legs, speed, and terribly loud buzzing sound give me nightmares. Mama says that I would unknowingly run in front of a truck to avoid a wasp. I'd much rather die by being run over than stung by a swarm of wasps.

Feb. 1967

I love to dance. I'd rather dance than eat. I wish
Mama had given me dancing lessons. I'm sure I
could've been a professional. I have a natural talent
for sexy dancing. I love to express my inner
tensions through the movement of my body to
music. It sure lets off a lot of steam. I have tall good
legs that would be good for dancing. I guess it just
wasn't meant to be.

Nov. 4, 2024

This year I choreographed 10 small dance routines for a music video with 15 of my friends and peers. I have friends who are great at dancing that have never taken a dance class in their lives. I took dance lessons for 5 years, but I've been dancing for a decade and I will probably continue to dance for a very long time. Mama took lessons for 12 years and yet she hardly dances.

Feb. 1967

I have such a bad back. I have been suffering so long with a bad neck and back. My chiropractor helps me, but it is expensive. I guess I'll forever have to go to him or else I'll just die of pain. When my back is having one of its spells I can't concentrate or enjoy anything. No one realizes how very important it is to have a good back. People with no backache trouble don't even realize how fortunate they are. I suppose I must accept my condition and learn to live with it.

Mar. 23, 2023

My hips keep partially dislocating. First it was the left hip, then the right, then left again. I don't know what I'm doing wrong. Is it the way I walk or sit or sleep? Daddy has to pop them back in place each time. This has been going on for almost two months. The pain is bad. Walking is excruciating. It feels like a sharp stabbing pain that runs from my lower back down to my thighs.

Feb. 1967

I live by the rule that whatever is meant to be will be. That all phases of our life and world are meant to happen for some reason. Sometimes things are hard to accept as meant to be. And yet we can look back at things that have happened and realize why they did.

I used to think everything happens for the best, but there are a few things lately that make me doubt this idea. Who knows what to think. Only the Lord knows and we're not supposed to know. We just must accept our lives and world around us and keep living as best we can. It is so hard to accept certain ideas and things in our sensitive lives.

Nov. 2020

Every year my Thanksgiving is spent with aunts, uncles, cousins, and grandparents. But this year is different because of Covid. I hate 2020. I've been robbed of being 15, I've been robbed of holidays, and I've been robbed of high school. It's my belief that everything happens for a reason and that nothing is random. Maybe I'm experiencing 10 years worth of bad luck condensed into 1 year, making the following 9 years of the 2020s nothing but perfect. I hope that's what it is.

May 1967

I am once again a complete person. My Daddy came home about 3 or so months ago. He wanted to come home and he promised Mama he would have no more affairs. So Mama decided it was time for him to come home and she wanted him to come home. He seemed to have his fill of living alone and caring for himself. He probably wouldn't admit a lot of things, but I know he's glad to get home. He missed all the comforts. Men are so ignorant and stubborn. He and Mama seem to get along a lot better now and have more companionship. They have gone on a few trips and are planning many trips in the future. Daddy has taken more interest in the house and the yard. He acts more like a husband and father should. He is healthier and looks better. His hobby is cooking and he really concentrates and loves it. I hope he remains or tries to remain loyal and be a better husband. You never can tell or put your whole trust again in a man who has been so un-loyal to his wife for 20 years. I'll never completely trust him again. No one ever will I guess. He is still drinking far too much and destroying himself little by little. Let's hope and pray he has the strength to regain his willpower and not drink so much. I love him. Mama loves him. We want him to live a ripe old age.

2022

Grandma has never told me that she loves me, so I have never told her that I love her. She shows me that she loves me in other ways. Mama said she just isn't the type to say it. Honestly, it might be really awkward if she said it. I don't know that we will ever say it to each other. She's like a wise old friend to me. We don't have a typical relationship like Grandmother and I do (if it can be called typical, but that's a whole new can of worms). Grandmother tells me she loves me all the time. She says it so often that I'm afraid it might have lost its meaning coming from her. But if Grandma were to say it, I wouldn't know how to react.

June 1967

Why are all men so ignorant? Women have to walk on eggshells to keep their men even-tempered. Women are spoiled and want to be treated like little girls, but men are worse. However, on the other hand men deserve to be treated like angels, sometimes.

Oct. 24, 2024

How I wish to speak to you again,
Even if only for a moment.
I am ashamed to admit how long it has been.
I have forgotten the smell of sun and your skin.
And you ought not remember the times we shared,
But I will remember for the both of us and recount
them when I see you,
If I see you.

I will look different then:
Older, stronger, and happier.
I will not speak nonsense to you;
My words will be clear.

We will meet like strangers for a second time,
And I will have another chance.

Then you will learn who I really am.
And the more you get to know me, the more you
will see how different my philosophy is from other
girls.

You will find that I do not get nearly as angry or jealous or controlling or shy or scared or uncomfortable.

I will be a breath of fresh air
For you to breathe me in and out.
I will be your vitality
As you are mine.

June 1967

I watch T.V. so much it is almost a sickness. If someone were to take a T.V. from me I'd wilt away and die. I wish TV had never been invented. If not, people would read more and be smarter. Families would talk more and men and women would be closer as man and wife. But on the other hand T.V. is educational and I have learned a lot of new things from it. It has its good points and bad. It has certainly brought me years of enjoyment.

Oct. 2023

I have my suspicions that Grandma is secretly a vampire. She only goes outside in the evening, is very pale, claims to be prone to sunburn, and stays up very late. Whenever I peer into her window I don't see her sucking blood, but I do see her watching T.V. Maybe she needs a different kind of plasma to live than that of blood.

June 1967

I am an old fashioned girl. I do not belong in this day and age. I should've lived in the Victorian era. I disapprove of the new sexual freedom of the younger generation. I do not believe in sex before marriage. I do not believe in smoking or drinking and for teenagers to take drugs is an unforgivable sin. I can't understand why teenagers are becoming so wild and immoral. I know modern times are more difficult than ever before, but you'd think teens would have more common sense. If teens are this bad now, what will they be when my children are teens? I'm almost afraid to have any children.

April 26, 2023

The day before yesterday Martha rode my bus to hang out at my house. These two rebellious sophomores sitting in front of me (boyfriend and girlfriend) caught a glimpse of me mouthing "I don't like them" to her. Whoops. They knew I didn't like them, but watching me say it made them mad.

Yesterday they were constantly looking back at me and whispering to each other. What were they plotting?

I don't like them because they are disrespectful, mischievous, and outright rude. I already emailed my counselor to get one of their friends suspended from the bus after his antics started affecting me.

Today the two carried out their little plan. They sat directly in front of me this time instead of a few seats up. The girl was flopping her back into the seat, making the metal sheet inside it pop in and out and in and out. It looked like the seat was breathing. Every time she did it the seat punched my kneecaps.

At first I figured she was just doing it out of boredom, but after a few seconds the pattern got more rapid and powerful. She was doing it on purpose to make me miserable.

So what did I do about it? I stuck my knee as far as I could into the back of the seat so that it jabbed her forcefully in the back when she threw herself into it. She screamed out in pain. It was well deserved.

June 1967

I love my mother's backyard in the summertime. It is so refreshing to look out the glass door and enjoy the greenery, flowers, grass and all the care my mother has put in on the yard. She loves yard work, but hasn't been able to spend as much time in the yard as she would like. She suffers from asthma, hay fever and back trouble. But in spite of some weeds and a few overgrown plants it is a beautiful yard, front and back. It is not an elaborate landscape, but the prettiest I'll ever know because my Mama planted it herself.

Mar. 7, 2023

Animals one might find on my property: dogs, cats, coyotes, raccoons, possums, skunks, gophers, tree squirrels, ground squirrels, rats, mice, blue belly lizards, skinks, king snakes, gopher snakes, bullfrogs, tree frogs, toads, freshwater clams, carp, bluegill, smelt, minnows, ducks, geese, egrets, killdeer, vultures, hawks, owls, bats, ravens, woodpeckers, invasive green parakeets, mourning doves, blue jays, sparrows.

Insects one might find on my property: dragonflies, robber flies, horseflies, hoverflies, butterflies, crane flies (also known as mosquito eaters or mosquito hawks), lacewing flies, black ants, red ants, velvet ants, Jerusalem crickets (also known as potato bugs), brown crickets, grasshoppers, katydids, praying mantids, cockroaches, earwigs, stink bugs, lady beetles, fruit beetles (or green June bugs), ten-lined June beetles (which I call hissing watermelon beetles), brown June bugs, water beetles, aquatic snails, regular snails, slugs, wolf spiders, house spiders, black widows, daddy long legs, scorpions, millipedes, roly poly bugs (or pillbugs), mosquitos, honey bees, bumble bees, carpenter bees, yellow wasps, blue mud wasps, black mud daubers, ichneumon wasps, yellow hornets, gypsy moths, black witch moths.

Oh, and one time I found a leech on me.

Aug. 1967

Summer has been hot this year. Long days of an average of 101° to 104° every day. Sometimes heat bothers me more than other times. I enjoy hot weather, but it has been too hot. Most of all I love warm nights. Nights that you can walk outside with a bathing suit on and you're just kind of sultry hot. I love that warm feeling on my skin. Now I seldom go out at night, but when I was a teenager it was wonderful to drive or walk with summer breezes brushing my face. When I am down in Southern California the days are nice, but the nights are terribly chilly. I hate cold nights. Soon fall will be here. Fall is such a nice time but I prefer spring for I'd rather see leaves coming than going.

Jan. 20, 2021

How fortunate I was to be able to attend the best middle school in the city. The only middle school with a pool. The only middle school that had the funds to take the 8th grade class on a field trip to downtown Sacramento for 3 days and 2 nights. One of the only middle schools to actually make their meals—occasionally with foreign and expensive ingredients—rather than have prepackaged pizzas or sandwiches shipped in. One of the only middle schools to have a fruit, salad, and snack bar. One of the only middle schools to give out free slices of assorted flavors of pie on March 14 (pi day). One of the only middle schools to have frequent dances, unrivaled competitive sports teams, a semester-long mandatory drama class for 8th graders to perform a musical at the end of the school year in custom-made shirts, a cake auction to raise money for the Sacramento trip, a boat race where students would construct flotation devices out of empty milk jugs to paddle across the pool, a marathon day where students were rewarded with different kinds of junk food depending on how many miles they ran, museum and amusement park field trips, and much more.

If it was your birthday you would receive a public shoutout from the principal during morning announcements.

During recess you could play volleyball in the gym, basketball on the court, football or soccer on the field, make up playground games, gather under a tree and gossip, hang out in a favorite teacher's classroom, or if the volleyball or basketball team was competing in a home game against another school you could go upstairs to the viewing area of the gym and watch.

In the days leading up to the school's annual sports relay you would practice a chosen event for every P.E. period to eventually be scored on the day of the relay. There was baseball pitching, volleyball serving, long jump, sprinting, relay racing, high jumping, and my choice: long distance baseball throwing.

And how cool the electives were. In digital media class you would be given a digital camera to conduct and edit on-campus interviews. My production crew would roam about the empty school halls while everyone else was in class. If we were to get caught goofing off we'd say that it was for the sake of capturing interesting content.

Mock trial was a lot of work, but I say it was worth it because my closing argument helped win the case for the defense!

Art class taught us the basics of color theory and had us making interesting crafts.

We The People allowed us to engage in lively debates and Socratic seminars.

Being the P.E. teacher's aide meant that I was responsible for overseeing the 4th graders and making sure they were on task. I would also have to clean or sort equipment in the storage rooms.

If you were a dancer (like I was) in drama class you would be asked to teach the choreographies of multiple songs to your peers.

My middle school was over 130 years old. A past elective offered was photography club which would utilize the dark room (now a storage closet) in the old gymnasium (now the library). Another was being a life lab monitor. Downstairs, in a large room that textbooks are now kept in was the life lab. There were enclosures for reptiles like snakes and lizards as well as aquariums for fish, crabs, and aquatic snails, tanks for small mammals like mice and hamsters, and bird cages for parakeets and such. A life lab monitor was in charge of making sure each animal had food, water, and a clean enclosure. This elective was cut around the 80s due to how costly it was. An elective I would have liked to take involved videotaping school performances from a small room above the auditorium. There were square holes of various sizes cut into the walls of the room for different cameras to record. The principal let me up into the now abandoned room upon request. I envy the students who got to experience such thrills and tests of independence. Middle schoolers nowadays are kept on tight leashes, causing them to rebel.

Along with the projection/film booth, the orchestra pit in the auditorium was closed off as well. How lame! Still, my middle school was the absolute best. My favorite part was swimming in the school pool for P.E. at the beginning and end of the school year when the weather allowed. Rather than change into our gym clothes and run laps, our exercise was achieved through participating in what was basically a grade-wide pool party. All 100 of us or so playing games, floating, swimming laps, or taking turns jumping off the diving board. There was a broken slide that would have been fun to use. I bet it's still broken. Afterward, you would rinse the chlorine from your hair and swimsuit in the showers, change into your regular clothes (in front of every girl in your grade because the outside stalls had no doors), and head to lunch.

Not every student was nice to or friends with each other, but there was a shared sense of community. We bonded over our appreciation for the rare privileges that we had as middle schoolers and the pride in our school that it gave us. Even the worst behaved students had the goodness to not jeopardize them and their classmates' freedom. They would own up to their misconduct and humbly accept the punishment.

I wonder how everyone in my graduating class is today.

1967

I live in a good neighborhood—all the people are decent, clean, all-American families. They have all raised their children well and keep their yards nice. The neighbors get along fairly well and we all get together often for potlucks, parties etc. I was and still am the oldest kid (not a kid anymore) in my neighborhood. When I was a teenager only about 4 others were teens but much younger teens. All the rest of the kids I baby-sitted for. Now all those "kids" are teenagers and all about the same age groups, so we have quite a lovely neighborhood now. Each year some are graduating from eighth grade and some from high school. I can't believe it when I see some of these so-called children behind wheels of cars. It makes me feel old at 23. I can't believe I've been out of school for 5 full years. I don't feel that old. I live next to the high school and see all that goes on so when school starts I see and hear all the activities and relive my school fun and sorrow. How can I forget when a football game nearly blasts me out of this house. We are so close we hear the roar of the crowd. There are times I wish for one day they could turn time back to my freshman year in school. I could spend one day visiting all the kids I knew. And so many of the poor kids I went to school with would be alive and not dead as they are now. I feel so awful when one of my school mates dies. So sad to die so young.

June 2024

Mama would get annoyed that all Grandma would talk about was her high school years. She "peaked" in high school. I did not. I hated high school with a burning passion. It sucked the energy right out of me. On multiple occasions I just didn't go to school because the pressure from assignments and drama with my frenemies was too much to handle. My mom would make random excuses for me. She'd call the school and say that I had bad allergies or I was sick. She could see how bad it was affecting me. I pity the people who "peak" in high school because they don't do much afterwards. I fear my brother Gavin is like that. He is Mr. Popular right now, but what about in a few years? He doesn't seem to know what he wants to do with his life. He isn't passionate about anything. He must know that he can't sit around and play video games forever.

If there is any phase of school that I feel so deeply nostalgic for, it's middle school: simultaneously the best and worst years of my life. I learned extremely important lessons there, and they've molded me into the person I am today. I still don't think I've reached my full potential yet. Will I ever reach it, or have I tapped a limitless well of improvement? I'm so curious about the future!

Dec. 30, 1967

Well, this is Dec. 30, 1967, and this dear old year is on its last leg. Each year that comes means a year less for everyone on earth to live. That includes me! I am growing older and I don't like it. I can say however that the older I grow, the more relaxed and settled I feel in life. I have more sense and more peace of mind. To me, youth is one of the greatest things in the world to possess, but what good is youth if you are miserable. It is better to be older and happier. To love and be loved in return is very important, but happiness is best. On top of this list is health. My Mama always said if you have health you have everything. I believe that, for what good would life be if you were constantly in poor health and ready to die. When I used to feel so unhappy as a teenager, Mama used to say I should be thankful I had youth and health.

Dec. 2024

Whatever happens, 2025 will be my year. I will make it my year. My last 2.5 months as a teenager and the first year of my 20s. The collagen in my skin will start breaking down, and I will get wrinkles. I hope I age slowly like my dad. He does not look his age at all. I hope I age well like my mom. She looks radiant for her age. I hope I live a super duper long life and get to see all the ways life will change with new inventions and stuff. I hope I don't get any diseases or cancer. I will eat very healthy in 2025 and take care of my body. Mama always says that you only get one body, so you should do your best to take care of it. She works in a hospital. Every day she sees where people's life choices lead them. She sees young people in terrible health and extremely old people in great health. I'm aiming for the latter.

1967

The most beautiful, wisest, greatest, kindest, most wonderful, most sensible, most logical, most unselfish, honest, truest, pure American, human person in the whole world is my mother.

Nov. 9, 2024

Our brown couch is not nearly as comfortable as our multicolor reclining sofa was. It collects dust in the shop building now. But I remember falling asleep on it, finding change in the cup-holding compartments of the armrests, and using the drop-down table to eat my meals with a show. It was the best sofa. The smell of Mama's conditioner was permanently infused into the head cushion of her spot from years of resting her wet hair on it. I often buried my face in it to smell her scent, especially when she was away and I was missing her.

Dec. 1967

I dearly love the Christmas season. The spirit, the tree, the decorations, the cards, the gift exchanging, the hustle and push of shoppers, the decorations on the streets and in stores, the lights on houses and trees, the sight of Christmas tree lots, and the fragrant, wonderful, once-a-year smell of a Christmas tree when you first bring the tree home. People seem to be friendlier and more generous. I love sending and receiving Christmas cards. If I was a very rich person I would buy all my relatives, friends and pets the most wonderful gifts they could imagine. I just wish I could have celebrated Christmas time in the "good old days" of the Victorian era when things were not so commercialized and fake. I hate fake Christmas trees. In those days Christmas was pure and real and not so fake and polished. When they had real trees and made most of their decorations themselves. Then, gifts were appreciated and not taken for granted. I wish it would snow at least on Christmas Day this year. The weather was warm on Christmas Day last year. How can someone get into the full spirit unless it's nippy in the air? It's too bad the spirit of Christmas doesn't last the whole year through. It would be a better world for everyone if it did.

Aug. 16, 2020

I don't often reminisce about my life before moving. In the early fall, Gavin, Lily, Denise, and I would offer to rake our neighbors' lawns free of cost just to jump in the leaves. We would swim in leaves and share our Halloween costume ideas.

Then when it came October 1st the family would spend the whole day decorating our house inside and out until dark. I loved the smell of the decorations, like cinnamon and plastic.

On the evening of Halloween our friend group would congregate at my house and trick-or-treat on our street. After which, we'd all jump in the car and my parents would drive us to church for their annual trunk-or-treat Halloween carnival. There they had a rock wall, train, bounce house, and various games.

When I was 11 I hosted my first Halloween party. It was a massive success (thanks to my parents). Way more people than Gavin and I had invited showed up. And it was all anyone could talk about at school the next day with our gross games, creepy props, music, and candy. Halloween will always have a special place in my heart.

Dec. 1967

I hope that the year 1968 is a better year for me and my husband, my relatives, my friends, pets, everyone, everywhere and the world will find more peace.

I hope this year brings Tim and I all the things we have hoped for. We have many things to be thankful for. Tim has a good job, we are living together in a nice house and our dogs are with us. Our relatives are healthy and safe, and we are healthy and young.

Dec. 2024

I can't wait for this stupid year to end. So much loss and disaster occured this year. It was a terrible year. Probably the worst year of my whole life. Will it only get worse from here on out? I hope not. I welcome 2025. I will make it a good year.

Dec. 31, 1967

It is exactly 10 minutes to 12:00, New Year's Eve, Dec. 31, 1967. This dear old year just has ten more minutes to live. I'm not at any party at all or doing anything. Just sitting here watching the clock. Someday I hope to go to a big fun New Year's party with Tim and dance all night. I never have gone to a big New Year's Eve party. Well, anyway, hello 1968. It always takes me a while to get used to writing the correct new year. I hope everyone who is at a party now is having fun. Won't be long until 1970. I feel old.

Jan. 2, 2024

I went to Martha's house for New Years. It was so fun. I've never celebrated New Year's before. My family doesn't because by that time we are still too exhausted from Christmas. Martha's family is fun to hang out with. They all live close to each other. She has a lot of cousins and good relationships with most if not all of them. I wish I could experience being family-oriented and having close relationships with my relatives, seeing them often. But my family is not very normal. I can't help but feel that I'm missing out on something vital. It's made me such a loner. Maybe I'm better off this way for some unknown reason.

1968

This Is All About Me - Marlene Ruby Bennett Robins

I Love: God and heaven, my parents, my husband, my dogs, my cats, my life, my relatives, my hometown, Delano, the San Joaquin Valley, California, the United States, dogs, cats, horses, all animals, mountains, forest trees, grass, nature, rain, indoor and outdoor plants, standing in the rain, running in a field, the smell of rain and wet earth, the smell of alfalfa and Christmas trees, Christmas and all holidays, warmth, spring, summer, fall and mild winters, spring blossoms on fruit trees, flowers, music, dancing, running, laying in alfalfa, walking barefoot, sleeping late, eating, food of all kind, fruit, water, milk, western and American Indian history, all history, Victorian era, Victorian houses, antiques, western movies, western clothes, cowboys, fairytale movies, princess movies, all movies, roller coasters, amusement parks, horse-racing, beautiful clothes, beautiful shoes, long hair, privacy, hot showers, parties, friends, painting, realistic, art, crafts, rocks, handsome men, riding horses, magazines, television, music of all kinds, old cars, parades, rodeos, celebrations, fairs, harvest holidays in Delano, the sun, a warm breeze, family gatherings, class reunions, swimming in warm water, picking wildflowers, writing and receiving letters, writing stories, baby animals, collecting dog pictures, collecting pictures of anything. I love old photographs, cameras, taking pictures, artistic photography, my parents' house and backyard, my parents' neighborhood, listening to my favorite singers, newborn babies, beautiful furniture, lovely linens, pretty dog collars, of the color of red, barns, stables, pine trees, willow trees, beautiful churches, right to worship as I please, freedom, security, love, sympathy, help, kindness, glassware, candles, books, ceramics, childhood, things that glitter, Hula dancing, pretty carpets, bright pillows, square dancing, colonial mansions, money, spending money, wasting time, dark hair, fairy tale stories, legends, wading in a cold mountain stream, panning for gold, having my back massaged, having my hair combed or touched, putting on makeup, putting on my favorite perfumes, beautiful stationary, good health, autumn leaves, listening to radios, good morals, baby leaves, swinging in a swing, walking in a park, sitting in the warm sun, hosing off plants.

Dec. 19, 2024

Things I Love: God, Jesus, praying and talking to God, my family, my friends, my animals, the ocean, the beach, sea creatures, sea shells, swimming, exploring, collecting, taking photos, making videos, editing videos, acting in skits, writing scripts, writing stories, writing poetry, fashion, eclectic homes, Mediterranean homes, Spanish homes, whimsigoth style, 90s and Y2K style, the moon, eclipses, the stars, shooting stars, sunsets, sunrises, rain, overcast weather, storms, pools, hot tubs, showers, baths, aquariums, freshwater and saltwater fish, my imagination, the color indigo, wearing maroon and orange, Art Nouveau, surreal art, postmodern art, making assemblages with found objects, repurposing in general, thrift shopping, the desert, desert creatures, plants and succulents, almost all bugs, big clunky junky jewelry, weird clothes, perfume, fireworks, quietness, liveliness, good chaos, family reunions, food, deep conversations that last for hours, receiving letters, laughter, spontaneity, getting lost in the moment, setting aside my worries, chewing spearmint gum, scary stories, ghost hunting, fantasy tv shows and web comics, my phone, the internet, social media, pop music, rnb music, rap music, Spanish music, the Spanish language, rocks and gemstones, traveling, Las Vegas, Los Angeles, New Orleans, California, Florida, learning about other cultures, shuttle rides at airports, hotel breakfast, trying new foods/drinks, dancing, choreographing, helping others, helping animals, nostalgia, Grandmother's house, soap, freshly shaved legs, summer, fall, Halloween, the fair, August, September, October, nonjudgmental people, supportive friends, finding lost items, cooking, baking, making new recipes, cleaning and organizing, warm summer nights and cool spring mornings, water balloon fights, gathering around a fire, playing board games, gift-giving, the mall, old tv shows, candles, going to parties, taking walks, playing hide-and-seek, the smell of a new car or new shoes, amusement parks, coffee, scratchers and gambling, dreaming, big cities, gardens, picking fruit, warm sheets, fuzzy blankets, sleeping, Christmas decorations, rewatching good shows/movies, getting my back adjusted, being recognized for my talents, receiving a strange or unexpected compliment, being listened to, being related to, my hair when it's straightened.

1968

These Are Things I Hate

I Hate: death, funerals, smell of funeral flowers, cold, being cold, the ocean, hate, coldness, evilness, people who are cruel and rude, silence, fog, starvation, diet, thirst, ring of a telephone, dirty people, dirty houses, people who dislike animals, people who are immoral and sinners, being pressured, homework, snakes, big spiders, sharks, any dangerous creature of the ocean, alligators, crocodiles, wrinkled clothes, mismatched clothes, modern furniture, modern houses, modern ideas, stuttering, stammering, the desert, cigars, cigarette smoke, alcohol, bad morals, people who don't brush teeth and don't use deodorants, boys and men with long hair, taking liquid medicine, shots with a needle, any kind of pain, fire, destruction, floods, hurricanes, opera music, abstract art, poverty, dope addicts, to see a tree cut down, being separated from my husband, pets and family, any kind of war, fighting, quarreling.

Dec. 19, 2024

Things I Hate: death, grief, being separated from my loved ones, war, bombings, shootings, murder, violence, human trafficking, rape, gangs, animal abusers, liars, thieves, crime, the smell of a dead body (don't ask), people who lack empathy, mean/self-centered/hypocritical/close-minded people, prejudice, racism, homophobia, misogyny, people who hate on other religions or political views, people who make fun of those with mental or physical disabilities, people who fish or hunt for leisure, people who hate and kill bugs, most men, arguing with my family, people yelling, diseases and conditions, recreational drug use, alcoholics, choking, drowning, depression, anxiety, loneliness, hospitals, being sick, shots, when my joints dislocate, cramps, constipation, gaining weight, road sickness, sunburns, any burns, cavities, headaches, stress, freezing up when I'm scared, reckless driving, being called names, being put down by girls, being shamed for human things, being ignored, acne, the smell of a dead skunk or stink bug, dirtiness, vicious animals, mold, bad breath, splinters, weird stares, scary and inappropriate dreams, posers and flakes, wasps, hornets, yellow jackets, bees, anything that flies and stings, earwigs, being bitten by mosquitoes/spiders/lizards, being allergic to cats, forced proximity with family, planes, disobedient children, crying children, cleaning up biohazards, being cold, broken nails, bad grades, boring places, when my food gets eaten, when my hair gets damaged, winter, spring, bell peppers, tomatoes, and drawing even though I'm very good at it.

Feb. 1968

Spring is just around the corner and I'm so happy because springtime is my very favorite season. The fruit trees here in the southland are barely beginning to bloom. In spring the air is crisp and I feel more alive. The winter grass is growing wildly.

2023

I like February. It's cold, but the sun shines brightly, giving me that nostalgic feeling of a cool August morning before the first day of school. I giddily await summer and early fall in February. It's my month of inspiration.

Mar. 1968

It is spring. My fruit trees are full of blossoms. Every tree has baby leaves beginning to grow. They are so fragile. I love to touch baby leaves. They make me feel young and I love to rub a baby leaf on my face. Nothing is more beautiful than blossoms on a fruit tree. Such fragile colors. If I could just be a tiny bit as good an artist as God, I'd be the best artist in the world. No artist can duplicate God's artwork.

Oct. 2024

There are so many things that we take for granted: the ocean, the ability to swim underwater, the ability to dream, the ability to taste and smell and see and hear, colors, the sunset and sunrise, the moon and stars, music, and scientific innovations like television, cellphones, fireworks, medicine, and amusement parks. God made space and deep oceans and the potential for scientific discoveries so that humans would never be bored.

April 1968

I wish I had talent to write good poetry.

July 2024

Those that say they hate poetry are just mad that they don't understand it. Poetry is beautiful. Maybe I will be famous for my poems or something.

1968

If someone would ask me why do I love animals so much I'd have a lot to say. I have loved and wanted animals from the day I was born. I have a lot of love in me to give to both human and animal. I love people so much such as my parents, husband and relatives. I don't love easy but once I give my love to anyone it is a great love. As much as I love my husband, parents and relatives I am shy at showing affection openly in front of anyone. I've always been that way. Yet these people know I dearly love them in all the other ways I show it. I'm just not one to kiss and hug much except I kiss and hug my husband, but not too much in front of people. I also need my husband, relatives and friends more than anyone knows. I think everyone needs someone in this world and if they don't I feel sorry for them. To me, almost as much as being loved I need to feel that I am needed by many people and many animals. I think when a person ceases to be needed they no longer have a reason to live. I think being loved and needed by people and animals is the greatest thing on earth.

That is a few of the reasons I love animals with all my heart. I want to love my animals and all animals and unlike my shyness with people, I can give and show great affection openly to dogs. I'd kiss my dogs a million times in front of the world. Animals return all your love and they love you no matter who you are or what you look like. And most of all animals need you. They need you for their complete care and life and I love to be needed and care for my animals or anyone's or all animals. I've owned all kinds of animals in my 24 years. I wish I could live where I could have all sorts of animals and not be restricted to household pets. If I were rich I would open my own private shelter for poor stray animals and if no one ever wanted them I'd feed and care for them for all their life. I feel so sorry for homeless animals that I could fall down and cry my eyes out. I could never go to an animal shelter and look at those pitiful eyes staring at me. I'd never get over it. I wish the Lord wouldn't permit so much suffering in animals. I pray to him to let all animals have a good life. I wish I could feed and care for all the homeless and hungry animals there are in the world. Of course I know that is impossible.

I feel sorry for people that are so selfish they won't even own a pet. I couldn't live without a pet. I am the happiest when I am surrounded with all my animals and more. I love them and need them and they love and need me and to me those are the most important things.

Jan. 4, 2025

My mom and I rescue stray dogs and give them homes. All of our dogs were rescued (besides Reno and Cassie who were born from Shay). Why spend money on a purebred or designer-bred dog when you can get any kind of dog off the streets for free. I don't understand this. You pay a dog breeder to breed more dogs when there are millions of dogs without homes already. It's ridiculous and infuriating. I will rescue any dog I can for the rest of my life.

April 1969

I have the best dogs and cats in the world. I dearly love my dogs with all my heart. I especially love my youngest dog Eve. It is unbelievable how much I love Eve. I hope and pray all my animals always live to die of old age cause I love them so much.

Dec. 2024

Reno is the best, most kind, sweet, funny, obedient, and understanding dog in the world. He is my soulmate. He gets me, and I get him. We are kindred spirits. Our souls are bonded. We can read each other's minds. There will never be a dog as good as Reno. He is one of a kind. He saved my life. He is an angel from heaven. I love him so much. We are best friends. If anything happened to Reno I'd crumble apart. If I didn't have a single person in the world who loved me I would still be happy because I have Reno. Even if we are miles apart I will still feel him. No distance can separate us. Nothing can.

April 22, 1969

I have an announcement to the world. I am pregnant! I'm carrying my husband's child and I am the proudest woman in the world. I am four months and one week pregnant. I am not showing as yet so it all really seems like a dream. It is a miracle to me for a woman to give birth to a child. The greatest miracle on earth. It seems too much of a dream for me to have a baby. I hope and pray I have a normal, healthy baby. It does not matter what sex. If it is a boy we will call it Shawn. If a girl we'll call it Shawna. We are very happy. It is due in Sept. I have a long time to plan and think about my baby. I hope if it's a boy it looks exactly like Tim. If it is a girl I hope she is pretty and brown eyed like her daddy. I am proud to give my parents a grandchild.

Dec. 2024

I have been thinking for a while: I'm not sure that I want kids. I don't want to be pregnant or give birth or have a baby or even a toddler. They are too much work. Too much time, money, stress, attention, and sleepless nights. I would not want to have a child if I could not financially support them. I could adopt a 3 or 4 or 5-year-old, but I would still be a little upset that the child is not genetically mine. I do want to pass on my traits. But I doubt I will find a husband in my life. I am very picky and I like being single. I think I am one of the very few people in this world who could die happy without ever having a boyfriend or husband or kids. That being said, I think I was put on this earth to do more than care for my relatives. I've made a pact with myself: If I get to the age where I can no longer safely have kids and I don't have a husband and I have the funds for it I will adopt and raise many children.

If by some miracle I do find someone that I want to marry, I will keep my last name, we will not have a wedding, and we will travel the world before even thinking about having kids. A healthy marriage is the foundation for a healthy family.

April 1969

I have such a wonderful husband. He is all I've ever wanted in a man. He is so wonderful to me and patient. He is good, kind, sympathetic, intelligent, witty, good common sense, strong, brave, religious, ambitious, athletic, outdoorsman, affectionate, understanding and all the good things that make a great man. I love him and I want us to grow old, old, old together.

Oct. 22, 2024

Dear Grandma Marlene,

It has been six months, and I haven't yet overcome my anger about your unexpected death. I'm not angry at you. I'm angry at everything around me. Because how dare the sun shine and the birds chirp and the plants grow and the people smile and laugh. Don't they know that you are gone?

I wonder how many people have thought that exact same thing on a day that I've smiled and laughed while they were mourning a loved one. Regardless, that is why I stopped watering your stupid orchid a month ago. When all the flowers fell off I waited for it to just die already. And yet not a single leaf has broken off or become discolored. It stands tall and strong and vibrant green. It's even growing more flowers I think. How is that possible? The bottom two leaves were wrinkled but not discolored at all. I watered it the other day and now the leaves are unwrinkled and firm and strong. I thought that only you could keep it alive and that it was just a matter of time before it died too, but I guess I was wrong.

I wish that you were given another chance instead of your dumb plant. Then you would still be here to take care of it, and I would be there to take care of you. I'm glad we at least got to say "I love you" to each other. And like I last said to you, quoting what you would say to me every time I left your apartment, I'll see you later.

Your Pisces twin,

Adrienne

End.

About The Author

Adrienne Walker is a pen name for privacy. The author is an avid artist, writer, digital creator, and dancer with a passion for fashion. She will study English at California State University Bakersfield to someday be a teacher.

In Loving Memory

March 19, 1944 - April 11, 2024

Obituary written by Shawna Walker

We are sad to announce the passing of our mom, Marlene Bennett Robins at the age of 80.

Marlene was the only child of Bart and Estella Bennett. She was raised in the McFarland/Delano area and graduated from Delano High School, Class of 1962. She married Tim Robins, her 4th grade boyfriend, after reconnecting after graduation. They were married for 52 years until his passing in 2016. Being a wife and mother was her greatest joy and what a wonderful mom she was. No one will love us kids as much as her. She lived in Porterville, Terra Bella, Bear Valley Springs in Tehachapi and Bakersfield.

A huge part of her life was her love of animals, especially the many, many dogs she had throughout her life. She also had cats, horses, chickens and many aquariums full of fish. She was a fantastic dancer, an amazing artist and a photographer. Mom was a lover of TV and faithfully watched romance movies, westerns, dramas, news and weather. Books, magazines and all kinds of trees and plants were loved by her. Her Delano, Class of 1962 reunions were some of her most fun times. Mom loved her Lord and Savior Jesus Christ and led a blessed and happy life.

She leaves behind her children, Shawna (Seth) Walker, Sheila (Elroy) Shields, Dan (Estephania) Robins and her grandchildren, Elle and Carl Shields, Adrienne and Gavin Walker and Caleb Robins. Her 3 dogs will greatly miss her too.

Services will be private in Porterville. A donation in honor of her love for animals to your local animal shelter would be appreciated. Even better, save a life and adopt a shelter dog.

If you would like to contact the author, send an
email to authoradriennewalker@gmail.com

www.ingramcontent.com/pod-product-compliance
Lightning Source LLC
Chambersburg PA
CBHW021647120626
46545CB00002B/742